Volume Four

BILLS AND BEAKS

Volume Four

BILLS AND BEAKS

Curtis J. Badger

STACKPOLE BOOKS

Copyright © 1991 by Stackpole Books

Published by
STACKPOLE BOOKS
Cameron and Kelker Streets
P.O. Box 1831
Harrisburg, PA 17105

Printed in the United States of America

10 9 8 7 6 5 4 3 2 1

First Edition

*Cover design by Tracy Patterson
with Caroline Miller*

Interior design by Marcia Lee Dobbs

Cover photos: Robin carved by Gary Yoder,
wigeon carved by Rich Smoker. Photographed by
Dan Williams, reprinted with permission from
Wildfowl Carving and Collecting magazine.

**Library of Congress Cataloging-in-Publication
Data**

Badger, Curtis J.
    Bird carving basics.

    Contents: Vol. 1. Eyes — v. 2. Feet — v. 3. Heads
— v.4. Bills and Beaks
    1. Wood-carving. 2. Birds in art. I. Title.
TT199.7.B33   1990   731.4'62   90–9491
ISBN 0–8117-2340-2 (v. 4)

Contents

Acknowledgments

A series such as this would not be possible without the generous cooperation of artists like Jim Sprankle, Don Mason, Mark McNair, and Martin Gates. Not only did they let me peer over their shoulders with my camera as they worked, but later they took the time to review the resulting photographs and to explain each intricate step in the carving process. Thanks for your patience, guys.

In writing this series, I have yet to meet a carver who was reluctant to share his or her carving techniques. The reason, perhaps, is that wildfowl art is a sharing process. Art doesn't exist in a vacuum; even the most talented artists have learned from others, and all the carvers I've met have been more than willing to pass along their expertise to beginners.

Not only are Jim, Don, Mark, and Martin gifted artists, they are outstanding teachers as well. Jim and Mark teach in the Ward Foundation Summer Seminar series in Salisbury, Maryland, and they conduct workshops in their private studios. Don and Martin have given private instruction, and Martin has been asked to join the faculty of a folk art school in North Carolina. Teaching is one of the traditions of wildfowl art, and each of these four artists carries on that tradition in an exemplary manner.

Introduction

The generic term "wildfowl carving" covers a lot of ground. It means different things to different people. To the waterfowl hunter, wildfowl carving means decoy making, the traditional carving of functional decoys from blocks of wood. But for nonhunters, it might embrace miniature songbirds, lifesize raptors, or even abstract sculpture.

Wildfowl carving in all its incarnations has gained a great deal of popularity in the last ten years. Although few hunters use wooden decoys today, more decoy makers than ever are carving traditional, working decoys. Of course, most are destined for the book shelf, not the duck blind.

The advent of precision, flexible-shaft cutting and burning tools in the mid-1970s gave rise to what is termed the "decorative" carving, as distinguished from the more functional hunting style decoy. Decorative birds, with highly realistic feather detail and painting, look real enough to fly away.

Carvers are now entering the field with backgrounds in art education rather than hunting or ornithology, and they bring to the field an exciting new brand of visual experience. At contemporary wildfowl art exhibitions, alongside a scrupulously realistic songbird, you may see an abstract form of a bird intended not to portray a certain species but to make a more personal statement about the poetry of flight.

Wildfowl carving has been with us for centuries, beginning with the spiritual totems of stone age hunters and extending through the golden years of decoy making in the early 1900s. But in the past few decades wildfowl carving has evolved to embrace not only the functional and the spiritual but the decorative and the celebratory as well. In the past few decades we have come to realize that our wealth of wild things is not infinite. We have discovered that our planet, despite its perceived vastness, is indeed fragile and limited. Perhaps that is why, now more than ever, we are driven to celebrate the beauty of wildlife in art. Perhaps it is our way of making permanent something we recently discovered to be transient and ephemeral.

Artists find different ways of celebrating their fascination with birds. One of the pleasures of working on this series has been the opportunity of getting to know many different artists, each with his or her own values, motivations, and vision. In each book in the series we have tried to provide a broad spectrum of experience. This particular book, on carving bills and beaks, covers approaches from the hunting tradition to the impressionistic. So here we have a narrowly defined subject matter, but a great range of methods of treating the subject. And that's what makes life interesting.

In art, we tend to reflect in our work the experiences that life has given us. Jim Sprankle became involved in bird carving after careers as a pitcher for the Dodgers and the Redlegs, a banker, and a business executive. While hunting in the Chesapeake Bay, he came across decoys carved by Steve and Lem Ward of Crisfield, Maryland, and immediately decided to take up carving. His birds, which are highly detailed and realistic, reflect the beauty of the real world, but they also express much about him and his life. You don't get to be a major league baseball pitcher by having sloppy technique. If your curveball hangs, you won't be around for long. And both banking and business are exacting pursuits that require attention to detail and mastery of the finer points. Jim's carvings are like this; they reflect, rather than an overall style, the mastery of a thousand small tasks.

Of the other three carvers in this book, Don Mason is most like Jim. Don is a young carver who has quickly gained a solid reputation with wins at the Ward World Championships and other carving competitions. His birds, like Jim's, are highly detailed and realistic. Don is an electronics engineer with the National Aeronautics and Space Administration (NASA), a job that defines the word "exacting." Before he took up bird carving he raced dirt-track stock cars, an avocation that leaves little margin for error.

Mark McNair's carvings reflect a variety of passions: Northwest Indian folk art, music, history, the hunting tradition, and old-world craftsmanship. His carvings are visually the least complicated of the artists represented here, but they may be the most complex in terms of what goes into them. They reflect Mark's interests in design, in decoy history, and in carving and painting technique. The curlew bill he carves is traditional in style and execution, an exercise in the pleasures of design and craftsmanship.

Martin Gates has only the skimpiest formal training in art, yet when he entered his first-ever carving competition, he won first place in World Class Interpretive Sculpture at the Ward World Championships in 1987. He brings to the carving process a fascination with old-world craftsmanship and tools, a background in restoring European antiques, and an appreciation for the wading birds and raptors that live near his home in Gainesville, Florida. A distillation of all three of these elements has made Martin one of the most successful and unique young carvers of the 1980s. Martin began his career working in his dad's antique shop, restoring antique furniture imported from Europe. Often a complex figure or a piece of molding would be missing, and Martin would have to recreate the missing part using traditional tools and techniques. He quickly mastered the chisels and gouges, and since 1987 his carvings have won major awards and have been exhibited nationwide.

This book is not so much a step-by-step instruction manual as a catalyst to help you discover your own particular vision and style. Art might begin with technique, but in order to grow it needs something that only you can bring to it, something that is yours and yours alone. So I hope that this series prompts you not only to discover something about the techniques of bird carving but to learn something about yourself as well.

1

Jim Sprankle
Carving a Cinnamon Teal Bill

Jim Sprankle is a perfectionist, which is one of the reasons he's won dozens of awards as a professional wildfowl woodcarver. Another reason is that he is an artist, and he brings to the carving process not only technical virtuosity but also a highly developed sculptural sense.

Jim's carvings are scrupulously realistic. An aviary is attached to his carving studio on Maryland's Eastern Shore, and Jim spends many hours studying and photographing birds before he begins a carving. These sessions help him not only to carve a bird with correct detail and scale but also to learn the nuances of avian behavior that give his carvings an edge in the competitions.

Jim uses as much reference material as he can muster. In addition to his aviary, he keeps a comprehensive file on every species of bird he carves. This reference material might include photographs, books, study skins, taxidermy specimens, and videotapes. He also uses plastic casts of heads and bills that show every bump and wrinkle. With such material, Jim is able to produce birds that are remarkably lifelike.

In this session, Jim carves a bill for a cinnamon teal hen decorative decoy. The bird is made of tupelo, and Jim uses a molded study bill, plus measurements taken from a live bird, to ensure accuracy.

Jim will use a variety of tools in this project. A high-speed grinder with a variety of bits will enable him to carve the bill accurately. A sharp knife and a burning pen will be used to etch lines and detail. Dividers will help transfer and check measurements with the study bill. And plumber's putty will create the membrane around the bill and nostril.

The artist at work: Jim Sprankle and his teal-in-progress.

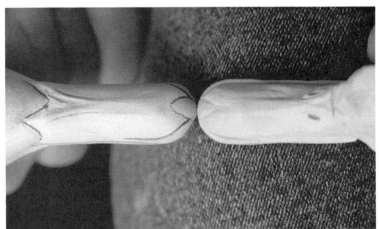

To ensure accuracy, Jim uses a cast study bill of a cinnamon teal, which shows not only the correct shape and dimensions of the bill but each small detail as well. In this photo, he compares the finished carved bill, left, with the cast bill.

The casting process yields incredible detail and is a valuable reference tool for carvers. "I don't know how you can do a realistic carving without references like a study bill," says Jim. "In competitive carving, we're judged on accuracy and realism, and references like this are invaluable."

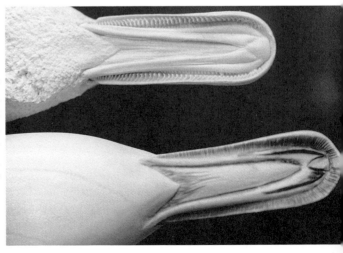

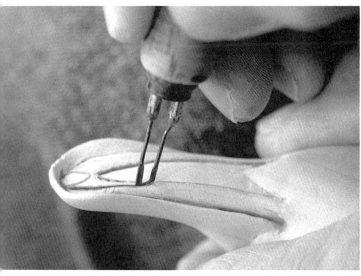

Jim uses a combination of a burning pen and knife to carve the bottom of the bill. He begins by using a pencil to sketch in detail, using the study bill as a reference. Then the burning pen is used to redefine the detail that was laid out in pencil.

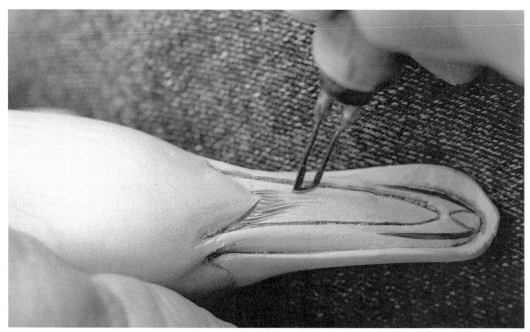

Jim uses the burning pen to put in the withered lines, or small creases, beneath the bill where it meets the head. The burning pen uses a sharp, hot tip to cut fine detail in wood. While the blade cuts, the heat slightly chars the wood fibers, producing a clean, smooth cut.

The same technique is used to create detail on the front of the bill.

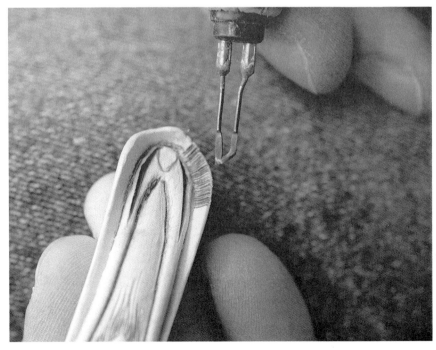

Using the study bill as a reference, Jim begins carving the membrane on the front of the bill.

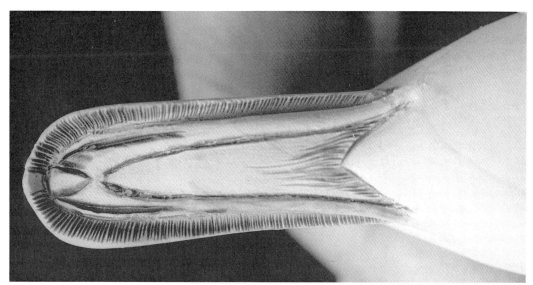

The bottom of the bill is finished. Jim uses 400-grit sandpaper to very lightly sand the area, removing the scorched wood left behind by the burning pen.

Now Jim moves to the top of the bill, using a pencil to lay out detail such as the nail, and to define curvatures on the upper mandible.

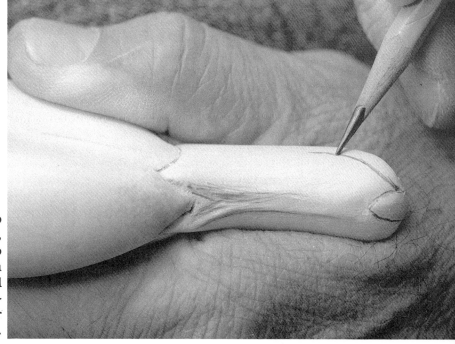

Jim begins carving the bill with a knife, cutting away most of the wood that needs to be removed. Here he follows the pencil line that separates the upper and lower mandibles.

The knife is used to do the rough carving, removing most of the excess wood. Later, the burning pen will be used to further define detail and to clean up the cut.

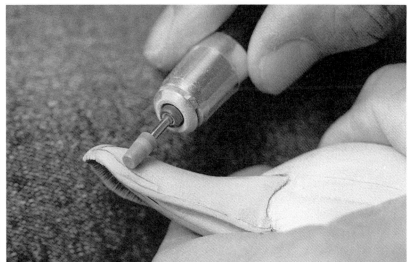

Jim uses a diamond cutter to shape the top mandible of the bill, again using the pencil marks and the study bill as a guide.

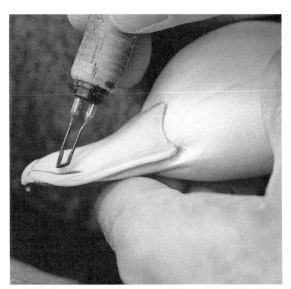

He uses the knife and rotary cutter to create most of the detail and the burning pen to add definition, as he does here on the nail.

With most of the wood removed by the knife and diamond cutter, Jim adds definition to the area with the burning pen.

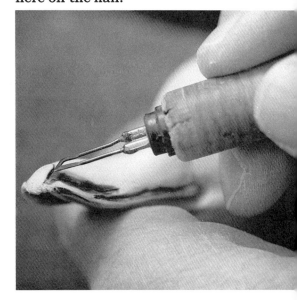

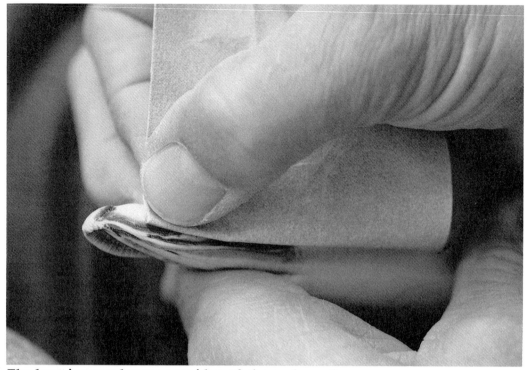

The burning pen leaves a residue of charred wood, which Jim removes with 400-grit sandpaper.

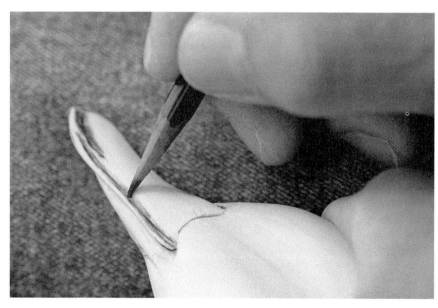

Jim uses a sharp pencil to clean the burned area on the bill. "The pencil," he says, "redefines the area and removes the grit, dresses it up a little."

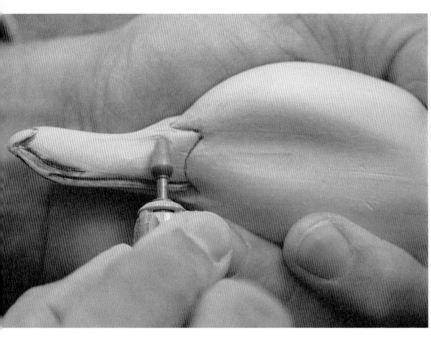

A diamond burr is used to shape the area in the upper mandible where the nostril will go. Jim refers to the study bill to obtain the correct curvature.

A ceramic ball is used to clean and smooth the area carved with the diamond burr. Now Jim is ready to locate and drill the holes for the nostrils.

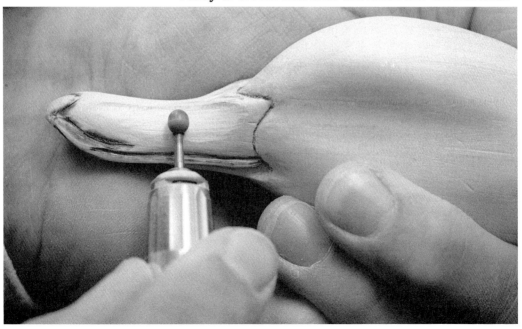

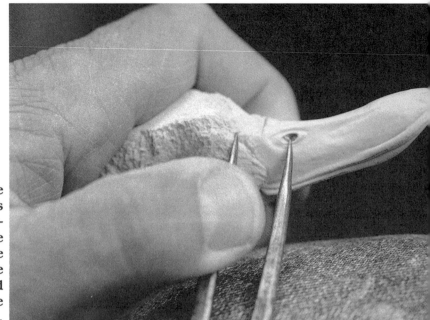

Jim measures the study bill with dividers to determine the correct position of the nostril. He checks the distance from where the bill meets the head to the center of the nostril.

He then transfers this measurement with the dividers to the wooden bird, marking the location of the nostril with the point of the instrument. The same procedure is used to locate the second nostril.

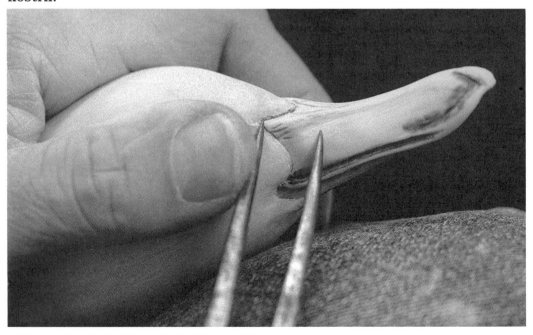

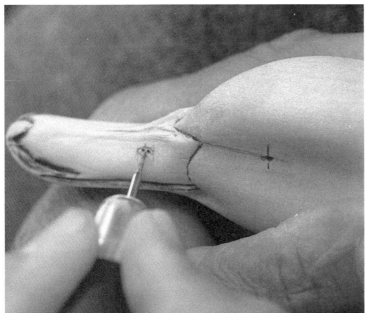

The shape of the nostril is taken from the study bill, and is drawn in pencil on the bill. Jim uses a small bit to drill the hole for the nostril. The hole is drilled from both sides and extends through the bill.

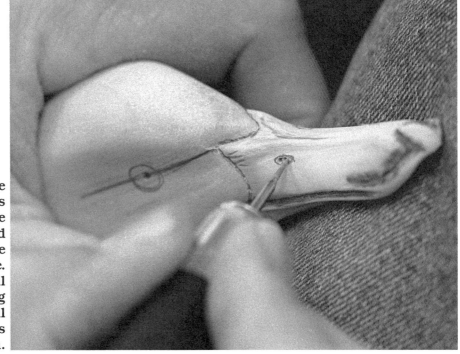

The bit in the rotary cutter is used to enlarge the hole and make it the proper shape. Note the pencil lines defining the nostril shape in this photograph.

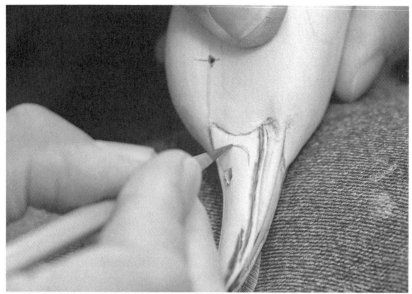

Jim draws the indentation at the rear of the upper mandible with a pencil (as always, referring to the study bill for location and curvature).

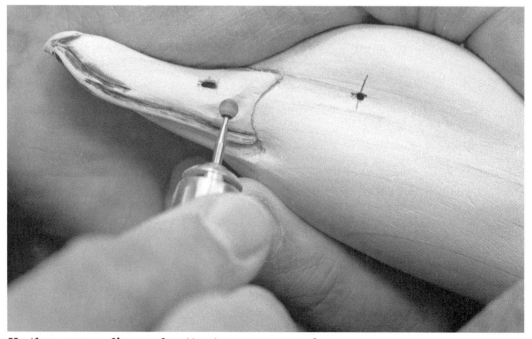

He then uses a diamond cutter to remove wood, creating the indentation where the bill meets the head. This step completes the preliminary work on the bill.

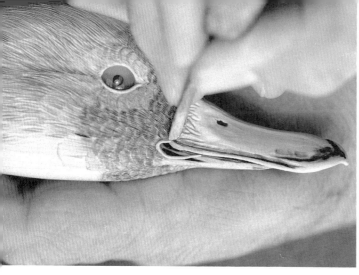

With the eye inserted and the head textured, Jim is ready to finish detailing the bill. He rolls out a thin bead of plumber's seal, a two-part epoxy, and carefully places it around the base of the lower mandible.

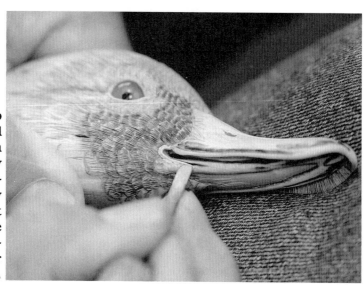

The seal is worked into place and smoothed with a small tool. Jim refers to the study bill for correct placement. Plumber's putty and similar two-part epoxy sealers are available in most hardware stores under various brand names.

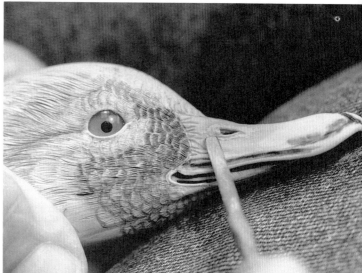

A similar bead of epoxy is also used to create the small membrane around the teal's nostrils. Jim uses the same blunt metal tool to press the epoxy into place.

The finished nostril. Notice how the epoxy
has been smoothed out to blend naturally into the
wood.

The completed cinnamon teal.

2

Don Mason
Carving the Bill of a Pintail

Until 1982 Don Mason spent most of his spare time driving dirt-track stock cars. When he wasn't driving them he was tinkering with them, attempting to squeeze extra horsepower from a souped-up Chevy.

In 1982 Don quit the racing circuit—too expensive, he says—and began looking for another avocation. That October he happened by the Ward Foundation Wildfowl Art Exhibition in Salisbury, Maryland, on his way to a race in Dover, Delaware, and he immediately became hooked on bird carving.

It's an unusual transition from stock car racing to bird carving, but that's the way it happened for Don. "I bought a copy of Bruce Burk's book *[Game Bird Carving]* that day at the Ward Show, and I went home and carved a bufflehead," he says.

Since then, Don has converted his basement into a carving studio, and the only remnants of his racing career are a few snapshots tacked to his studio wall. His home, which overlooks the seaside marshes of Virginia's Eastern Shore, is filled with his carvings and ribbons won at a variety of carving competitions.

Don, who works in electronics at NASA, took a workshop with Pat Godin in Salisbury in 1985, and has worked diligently at developing his technique. For the past two years he has competed in open (professional) class and has chalked up wins at the Ward World Championship in Ocean City, Maryland, at the Mid-Atlantic in Virginia Beach, and at shows in Richmond, Chestertown, Maryland, and Tuckerton, New Jersey.

Don specializes in realistic birds and uses a wide variety of reference material, including cast study parts, photographs, and videotapes.

In this session he carves a bill for a decorative pintail drake, beginning the process with a detailed sketch he will use as a pattern. The sketch is done freehand with the aid of reference material, primarily color photographs. This session continues in volume three of this series, in which Don carves and textures the head of the pintail drake.

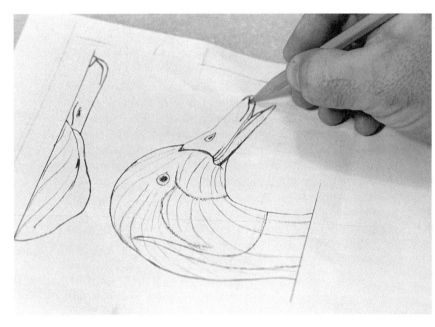

Don begins the pintail head and bill by drawing a pattern, using as reference color slides and a cast study bill. He draws both the side and top view and adds as much detail as possible, including positions of eyes and nostrils, the nail on the bill, and the flow lines of feathers. Note that this pintail will have an open bill.

Once the pattern is drawn, Don cuts it out and transfers the detail to wood.

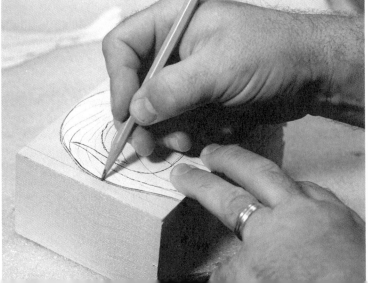

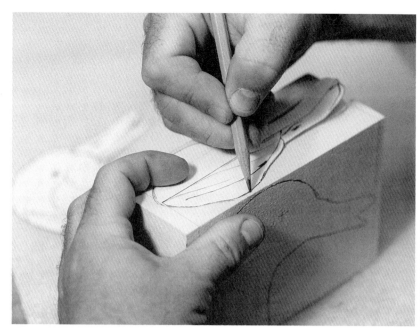

He also draws the top pattern, transferring bill detail and feather flow lines to the wood.

Don first cuts the top view on the bandsaw, then the side view. This method gives him more accuracy in bill placement and detail. He cuts the bill width very close to the finished width on the bandsaw.

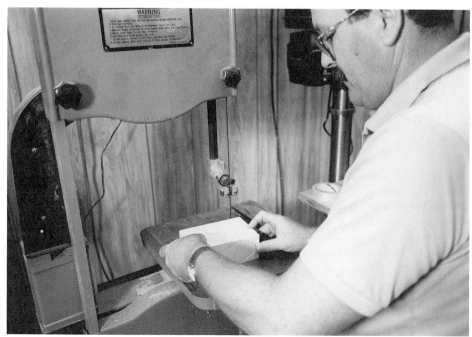

Once the head is roughed out, Don uses a pencil to draw a center line around the entire head and bill.

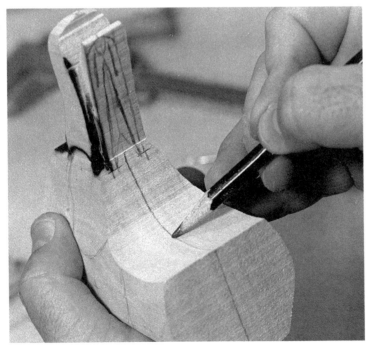

The center line is very important because it represents the high point of the carving and it will be an important reference later when the head and bill are rounded off.

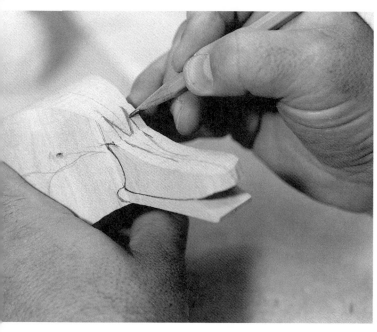

The next step is to draw in the bill detail. Here Don sketches the area where the bill meets the head, drawing the width of the bill at that point.

Don prefers to use a burning tool to carve bill detail. "I've found that I have more control with the burning tool than with the knife or grinder," he says. "It gives me a good, flat cut and a good surface to work with."

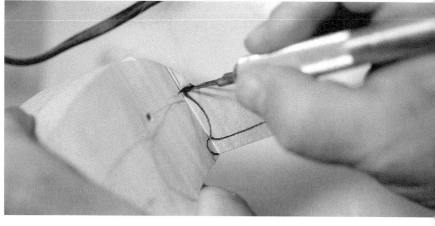

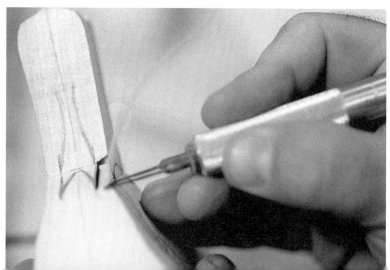

Don uses the burning tool, which he made himself, to backcut the area where the bill meets the head.

19

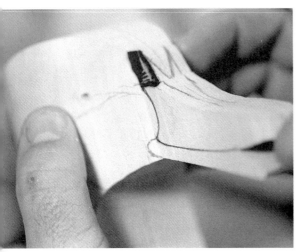

Don then uses the tool to make a reference cut at the edge of the bill along the bottom of the upper mandible. The pencil line he is following was drawn in from the original pattern.

When this cut is done, he will have established the width of the upper portion of the bill.

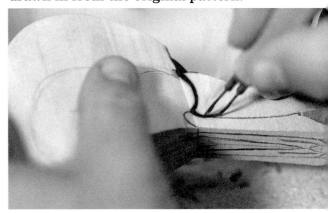

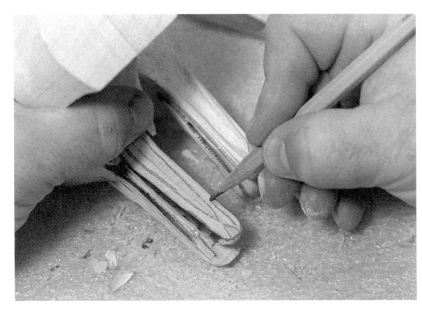

Don sketches detail under the bill using the cast study bill as a reference.

He then turns the head over and uses the burning tool to make a cut on the side of the lower mandible. This cut, in combination with the one made along the edge of the bill, will define the area where the upper and lower mandibles meet.

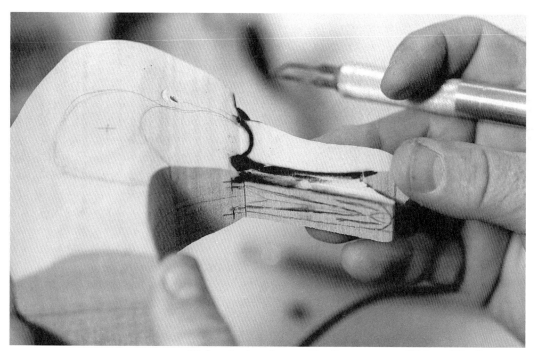

This photo shows the lower mandible with the wood removed from the previous two cuts. The lower mandible is considerably narrower than the upper mandible and actually fits inside it when the bill is closed.

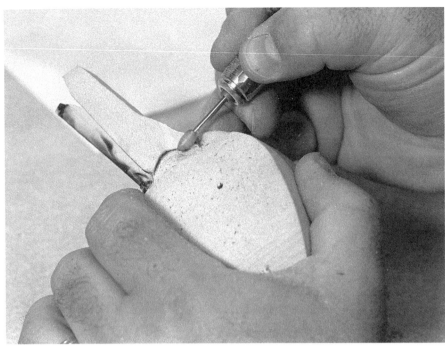

Once both sides of the bill are roughed out, Don uses a ruby cutter on a high-speed grinder to taper the bill from the tip to the reference marks where the bill meets the head.

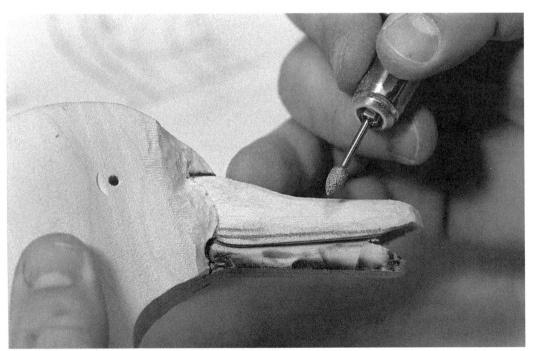

The ruby carver is also used to round off the bill. Leave plenty of wood around the nostril and nail areas. Note that Don has sketched the narrow "lip" along the lower part of the top mandible.

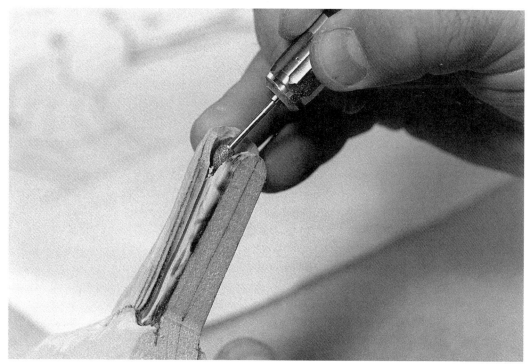

With the ruby cutter and high-speed grinder, Don begins to create the separation between the upper and lower mandibles.

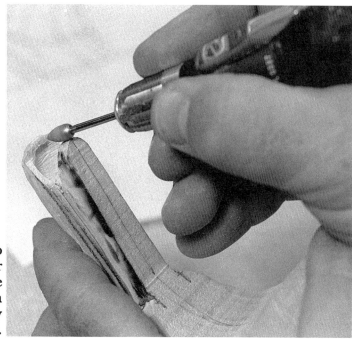

The same cutter is used to round off the end of the lower mandible. The length of the lower mandible should be such that it will be overlapped by the nail on the upper mandible.

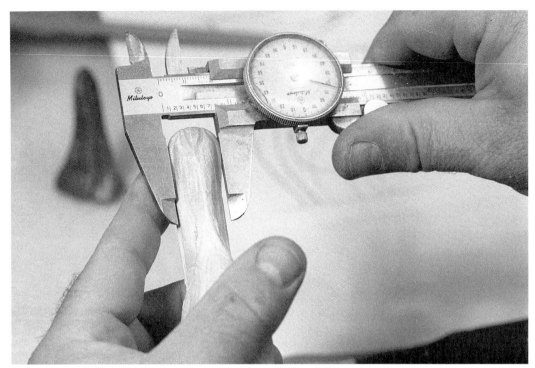

Don uses dial calipers to measure the width of the study bill.

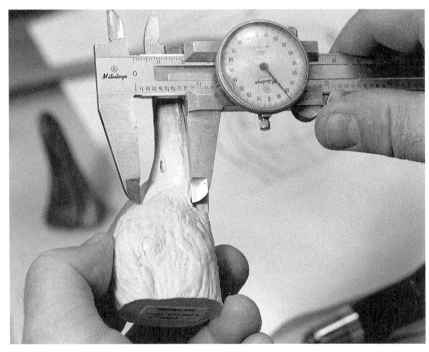

He also measures the thickness of the upper mandible where it joins the head.

These measure-ments are trans-ferred to the workpiece to ensure that the width and thick-ness of the bill are correct.

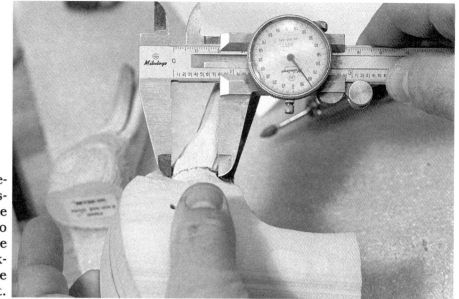

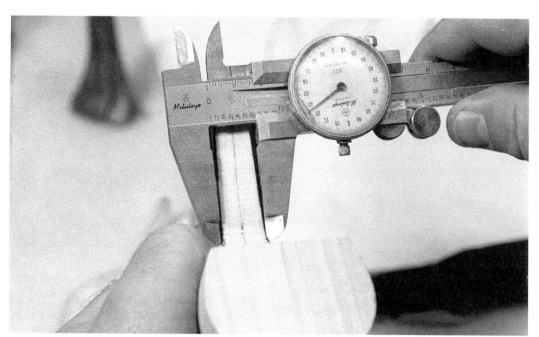

Here Don uses the calipers to check the width of the lower mandible. If dial calipers are not available, the measurements can be transferred with dividers or similar tools.

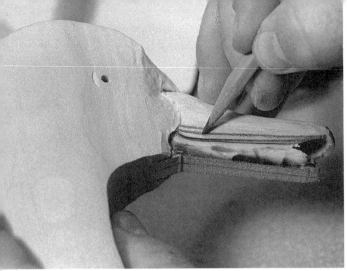

There is a slight ridge, or lip, on the lower part of the upper mandible, which Don is sketching in this photo. There is also a second small ridge, or wrinkle, just at the base of the bill, above the lip.

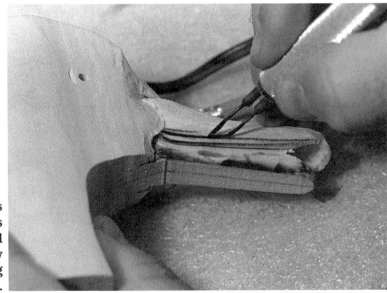

With the lines drawn in, Don uses the burning tool to cut a shallow groove along the pencil line.

Here Don cuts a groove along the "wrinkle line" above the lip.

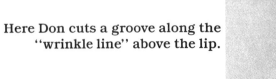

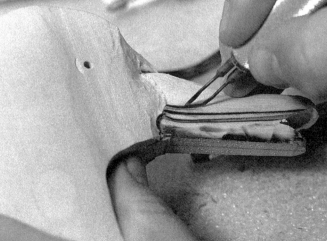

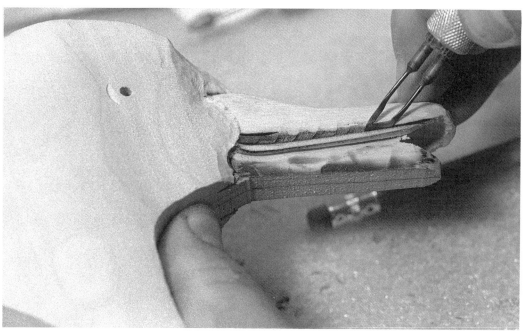

Don uses the side of the burning tip to round off the edge of the groove along the upper mandible. This step will make the ridge slightly more pronounced.

A small, pointed diamond tip is used to round off and smooth the groove on the bottom of the upper mandible.

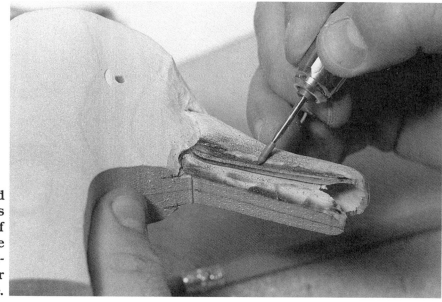

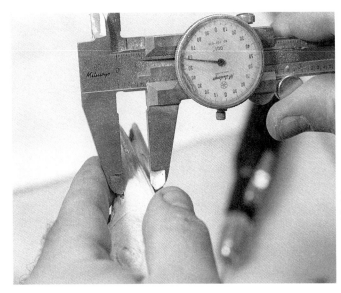

Now Don is ready to locate the nostrils. He uses the dial calipers to measure on the study bill the distance from the middle of the nostril to the bottom of the upper mandible.

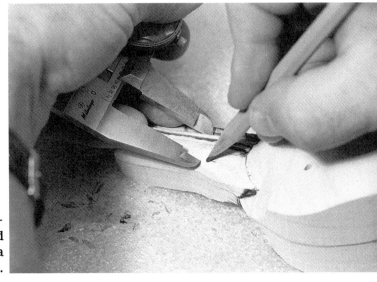

He transfers this measurement to the workpiece and draws a small line with a pencil.

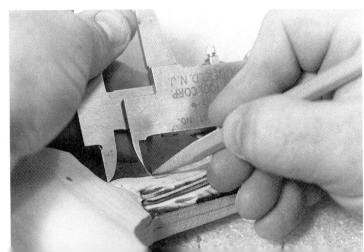

Don also measures on the study bill the distance to the nostril from where the bill meets the head and transfers this measurement to the workpiece. The correct placement of the nostril will be where this line crosses the line made in the previous step.

Don uses a long, narrow burning tip to burn into the bill from both sides. This opening will serve as the reference point for carving nostrils.

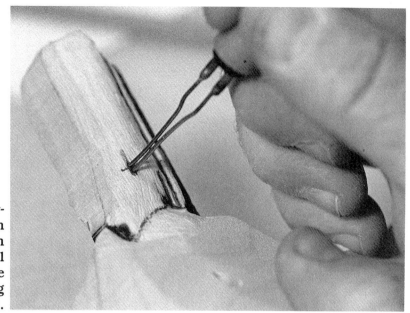

Once the nostrils are located, Don uses a gouge to cut away wood along both nostrils until that area of the bill is the proper width. The study bill is used to check this dimension.

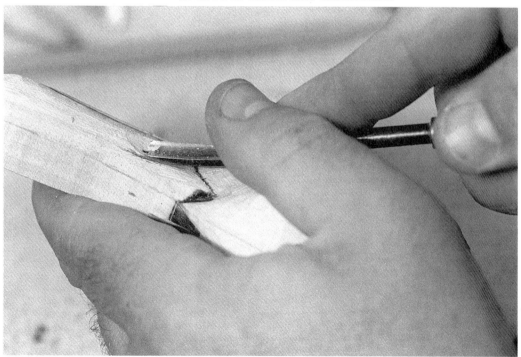

Don uses a pencil to
sketch the rim
around the nostrils.

At this time he also sketches the area on the front
of the bill where the nail is located. A slight ridge
runs around the front of the bill, and this is
marked with pencil, again using the study bill as
reference.

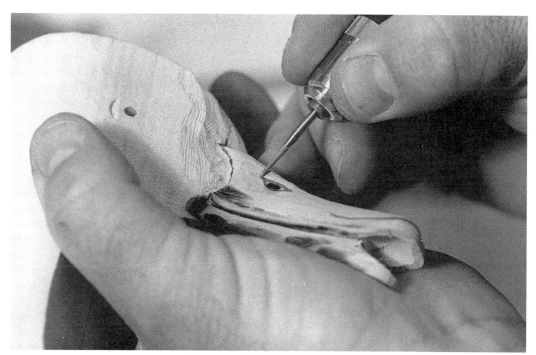

To create the ridge around the nostrils,
Don uses a small, pointed diamond cutter to
undercut the wood just outside the ridge.

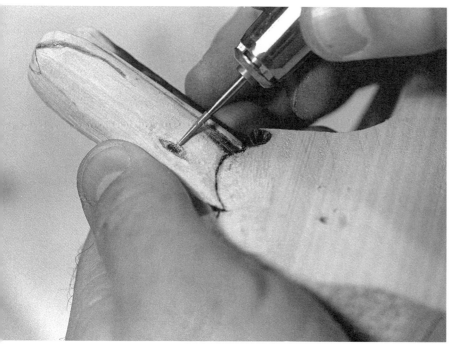

The same tool is
used to create
a raised area along
the bottom of
the nostril.

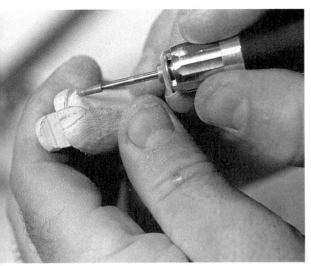

The ridge is rounded off with the diamond cutter. This tool also is used to define the nail, which should protrude down slightly.

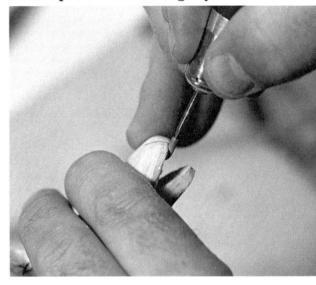

Don uses a slightly larger diamond cutter on the high-speed grinder to begin carving the nail area. Here he defines the ridge that begins at the nail and extends along the side of the bill.

The same diamond cutter is used to remove wood from the inside of the bill and to shape the inside of the upper mandible and the tongue.

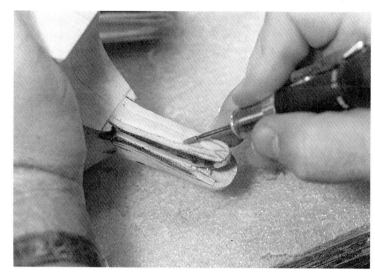

A small diamond cutter is used to add detail under the bill. The bottom of the bill has a slight V shape.

Don sometimes uses a larger, pointed ruby cutter to carve the area under the bill. This bit removes wood faster, but will not carve fine detail as will the smaller diamond cutter.

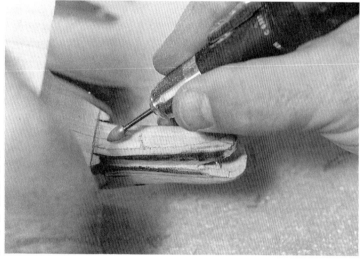

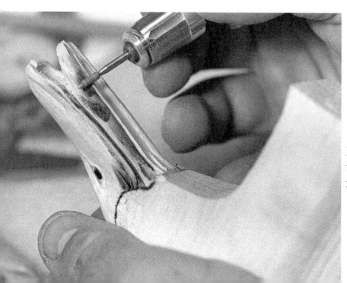

Next he rounds off the sides of the lower mandible with the diamond cutter.

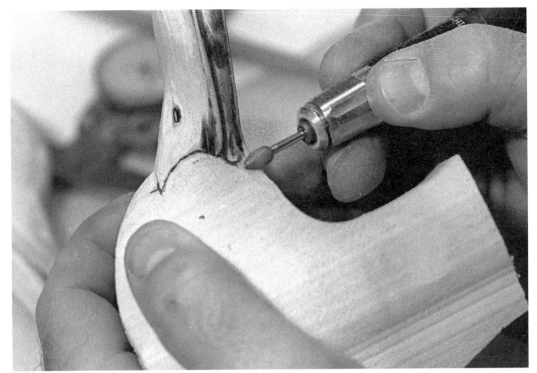

The ruby cutter is used to remove wood where the
lower mandible meets the upper mandible.
Because the lower mandible is narrower, the area
of the head just behind the mandible should be
tapered slightly.

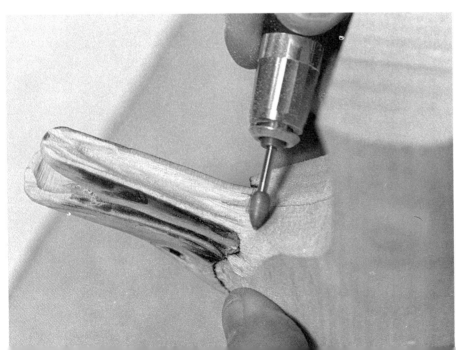

The ruby cutter
is used to
shape the wood
under the bill,
creating a
smooth transi-
tion where the
bill meets the
neck.

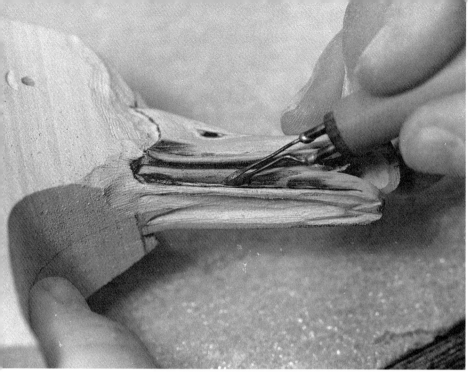

With the bill roughed out, Don uses the burning tool to define the serrated membrane along both mandibles, referring to the cast study bill to make it as realistic as possible.

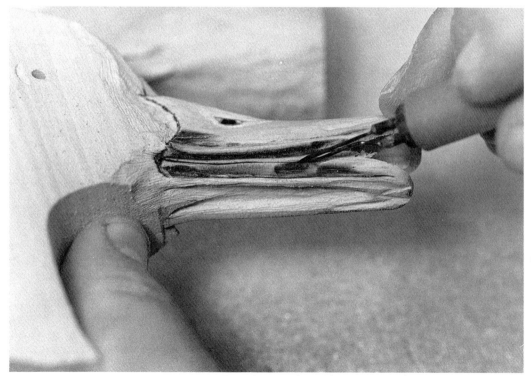

Here Don burns in a line separating the tongue and the lower mandible.

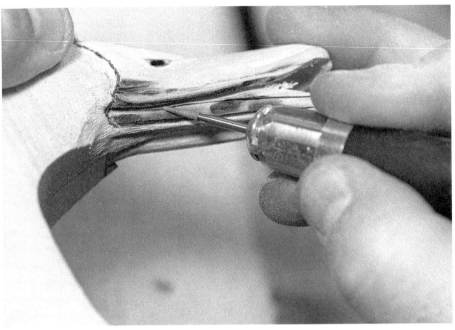

The pointed diamond grinder is used to round off the line Don just cut with the burning tool. This will create a slight groove where the tongue and lower mandible meet.

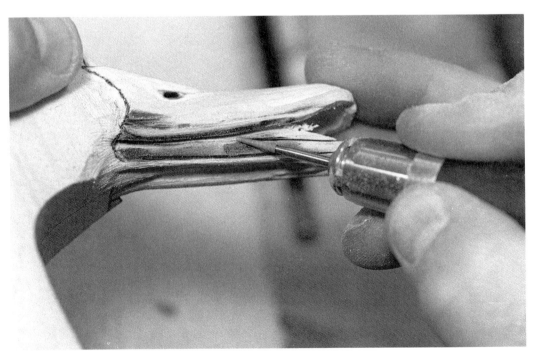

The line defined by the diamond cutter also creates the filtering membranes along the edges of the bill. The duck uses these membranes when feeding. This area will be serrated with the burning tip later in the carving process.

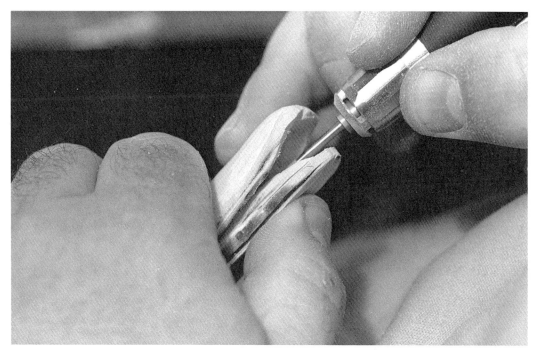

Now Don goes back to the bill opening, shaping the inside of the upper mandible. The center of the upper mandible has a small ridge running down it, which corresponds to a slight depression in the tongue. Don uses the diamond cutter to carve this ridge, removing wood on both sides of it.

The ruby cutter is now used to shape the tip of the tongue at the end of the lower mandible.

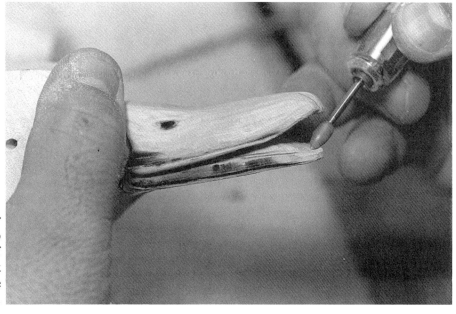

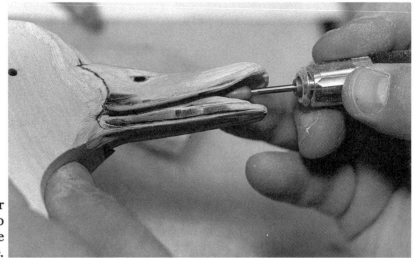

The ruby cutter also is used to cut the groove in the tongue.

Now Don goes back to the burning tool to begin cutting the serrations that line the lower mandible.

The serrations extend from tip of the bill all the way to the base. Note that Don has also used the burning tool to define the nail.

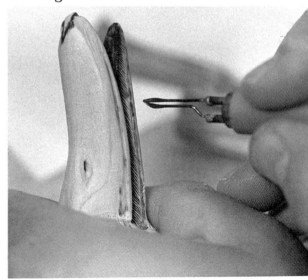

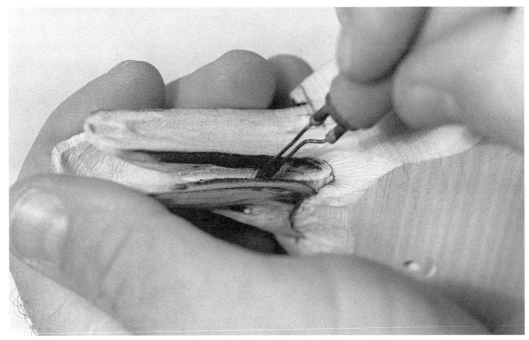

Here the burning tool is used to separate the tongue from the upper mandible in the back portion of the bill where it meets the head.

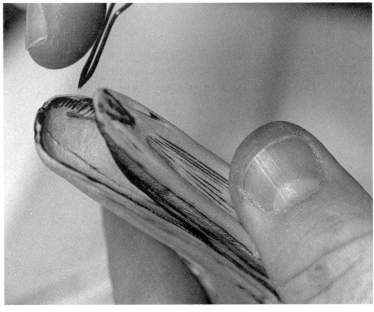

Serrations are added to the edges of the upper mandible on both sides of the bill.

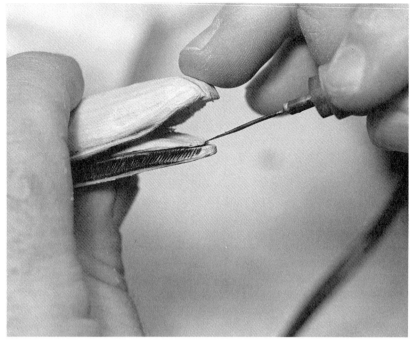

Here Don uses the burning tool to make a slight separation between the tip of the tongue and the lower mandible, creating the illusion that the tongue is lying on the lower mandible. The detailing is now complete; the bill is ready for a light sanding and paint.

The finished pintail drake.

3

Mark McNair
Carving and Inserting a Curlew Bill

Mark McNair grew up in Connecticut and moved to the Virginia coast some twelve years ago. It is ironic, though unintended, that Mark's move to Virginia was very similar to that of one of his predecessors in wild-fowl art, a Massachusetts shipbuilder named Nathan Cobb.

Cobb moved from New England to Virginia in the 1830s, almost 150 years before Mark did. Cobb settled in a little town called Oyster and later purchased a coastal island where he carved decoys and ran a sportsman's hotel. Mark has no plans for a hotel, but he came to Virginia at about the same age Cobb did, and like Cobb, Mark spends his days making incomparable decoys in the hunting tradition. Mark lives on a farm overlooking Currituck Creek, some thirty miles northwest of where Nathan Cobb eventually settled.

Mark admires Cobb's craftsmanship and his ability to capture the essence of a bird with a minimum of detail. You see a lot of this in Mark's work; this minimalist practice of using the smallest gesture to capture something universal about a bird. But there's more. Mark is influenced by Northwest Indian art, by music, by history, by all the visual arts. His carvings are clean, graceful, and uncluttered, but they come from something more complex than they seem to. Mark's carvings are a melting pot of visual experience.

In this session he carves and inserts a bill for a curlew, a common wading bird along the Virginia coast where he lives. In the late 1800s and early 1900s, curlews and other shorebirds were regularly hunted, and decoys such as this were used extensively in the marshes around Cobb Island. This bird is crafted in the Nathan Cobb style, and the bill, which is made of white oak, is inserted through the head and wedged in place at the back of the head.

Mark carves the bill from seasoned white oak. "It's tough and easy to work, just the qualities I need for making a bill." Mark uses the bandsaw to cut a piece of oak from a split log.

Mark cuts a section approximately two inches wide, half an inch thick, and eight inches long. To provide strength, the grain should run parallel with the length of the bill. When the block has been cut, Mark sketches the approximate shape of the bill.

The bill will be inserted into the head with a mortise and tenon joint. The tenon, which Mark is cutting here, should be the length of the head or slightly longer because it will extend through the head and be flush with the back of the head.

The tenon is square at this stage in the carving process. It will later be rounded. Mark will save a small chip of oak for later use as a spline to make the mortise-tenon joint permanent. "Essentially, what I'm doing here is putting two pieces of wood together so they become one. I've found that this is a superior technique, although it's by no means the only one. It gives a beautifully finished joint and is a very satisfying procedure."

Mark uses a knife to refine the saw cut; the surface of the bird's face and the shoulder of the
tenon must match perfectly. "If you take your time
with the saw and you're careful, cleanup should
be minimal. The important thing is to ensure that
the tenon and the plane of the face are perpendicular. Otherwise you'll be chasing angles all day.
You have to keep things straight."

Mark uses a $9/32$-inch
drill bit to create
the mortise. Here he
compares the bit size to
the thickness of the
tenon; they should be
identical. Before the
tenon is inserted, it will
be rounded.

Now Mark is ready to determine the bill position and drill the hole for the mortise. He begins by drawing a line along the side of the head perpendicular to the face of the bird.

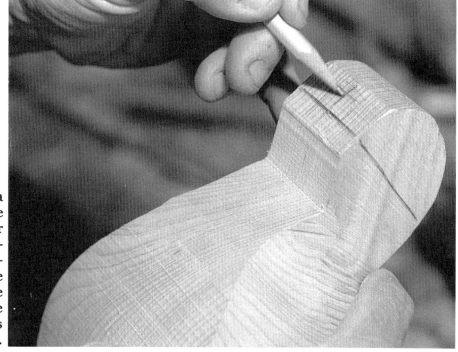

Mark draws a vertical line along the center of the face bisecting the horizontal line. The hole will be drawn where these two lines intersect.

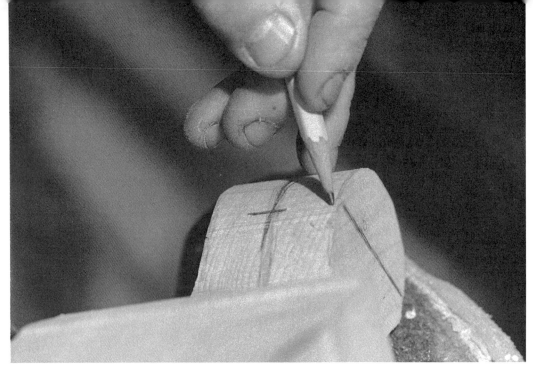

In the same way he establishes the exit point for the drill bit on the back of the head. The lines along the side and top of the head will help Mark keep the bit in proper alignment as he drills, ensuring that the mortise is perpendicular to the face.

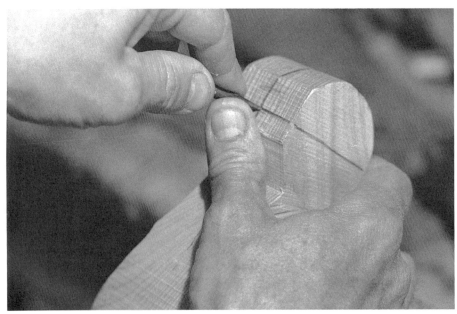

He uses an awl to make a pilot hole for the drill bit.

Mark drills the mortise slowly and carefully, making sure that the bit is perfectly aligned with his markings. It's important to use a sharp bit and ease it through the wood, he says. If you try to force a dull bit through, it may cause the wood to split as it exits.

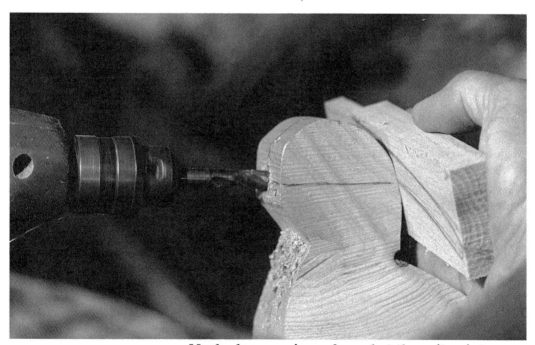

Mark places a piece of wood at the exit point on the back of the head to prevent the wood around the hole from tearing when the drill bit emerges.

With the hole bored, the tenon is checked for size. It must now be rounded to fit the mortise.

Mark begins rounding the tenon by using a knife to chamfer the edges, making it eight-sided. Mark will not round the entire length of the tenon, but will instead keep square approximately one-quarter inch of the tenon at its base. This will add strength to the bill and prevent it from rotating after it has been inserted.

"Control is the name of the game," he says, "especially with this joint. You first chamfer the edges to establish the diameter and keep it true. The rasp finishes the job nicely." To illustrate, Mark has sketched the chamfering and rounding process on the side of the workpiece.

With the tenon rounded (except for the quarter inch at the base), Mark tests the fit.

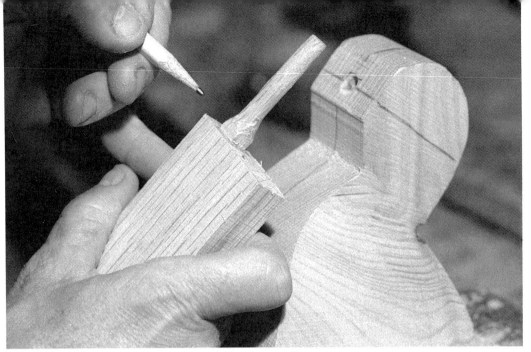

Now that the rounded portion of the tenon fits,
Mark will square off the front of the mortise to
accept the square portion of the tenon. This photo
shows the shape of the finished tenon. The
square base will prevent the bill from rotating and,
because it is thicker, provides strength at the
critical joint between bill and head.

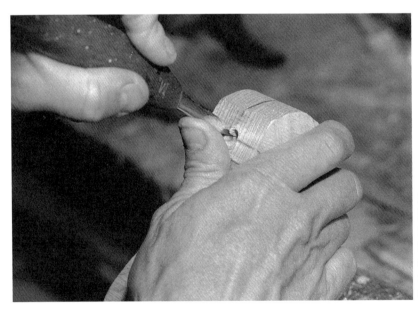

Mark uses a
knife to square
the front of
the mortise to
accommodate
the square base
of the tenon.

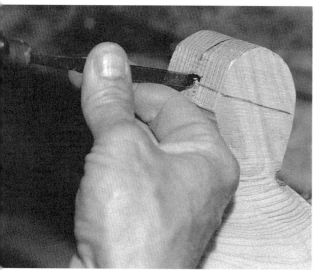

A bench chisel is used to clean out the excess wood.

Now the bill is rough-fitted, with the square base of the tenon fitting into the mortise.

The fit should be tight, and Mark uses a light mallet to tap the bill into place. "You don't want to force it, or you'll split the head," he says. "If it's right, it will move with a few light taps."

Now Mark draws the bill. "At this point, I can look at the bird in total. I can look at the shape and angle of the head, and I can visualize where the eyes should be placed. I have ample material with which to develop the bill, to move it slightly up or down or sideways. That's why I use ample wood."

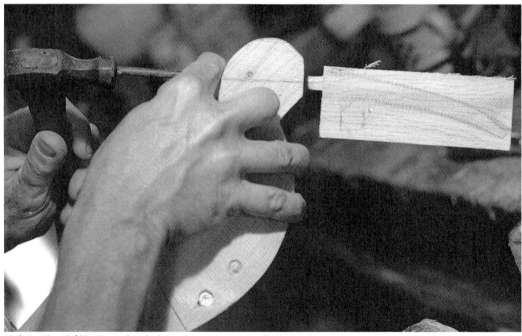

With the bill sketched, Mark uses a mallet and a small rod to remove the bill from the head.

The bill goes back to the bandsaw, where the profile is cut.

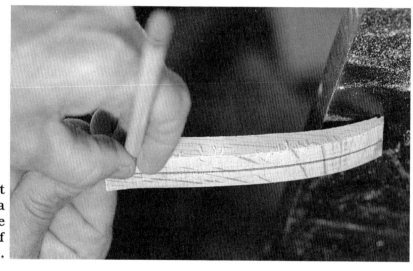

Mark's next step is to draw a center line down the top of the bill.

The sides of the bill are parallel, so Mark draws two pencil lines representing the outside dimensions of the bill. His fingers act as a gauge.

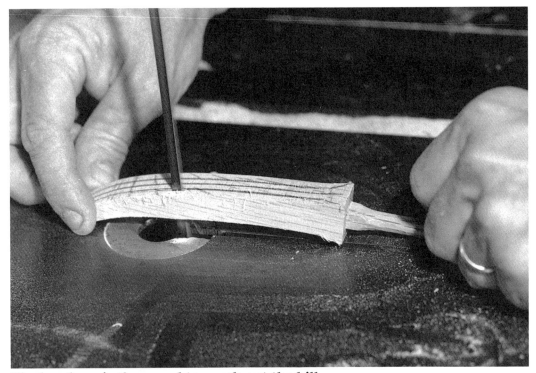

The bandsaw is then used to rough out the bill.
Notice that the bill flares slightly at its base.

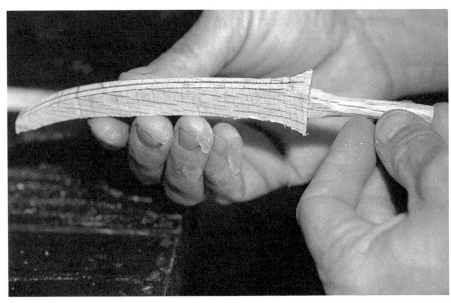

The roughed-
out bill, showing
the tenon and
the flared
surface where
the bill will meet
the head.

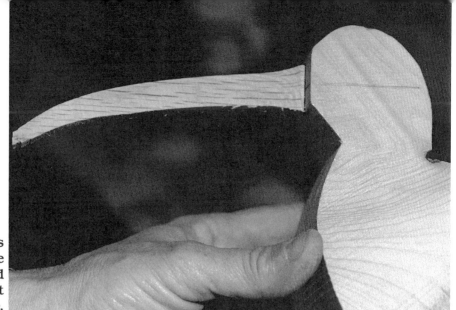

The bill is replaced on the bird and checked for a tight fit at the interface.

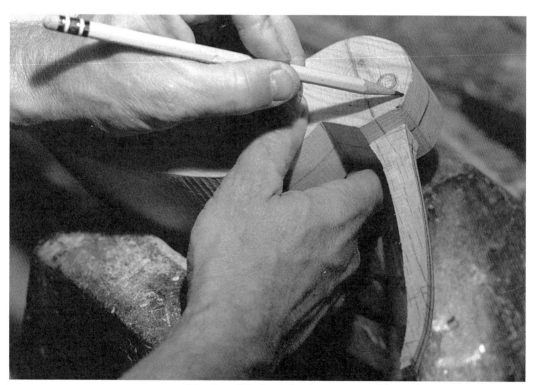

Mark will sketch the eye at this point and draw additional detail on the head. The pencil is used here to plan the knifework that will come in succeeding steps.

The bill and the head can now be worked as one. The large skew chisel is used to further define the cheek area where it meets the base of the bill.

The head has been cut to shape and the fit is checked. The surfaces of the bill and face fit tightly, with no seams evident.

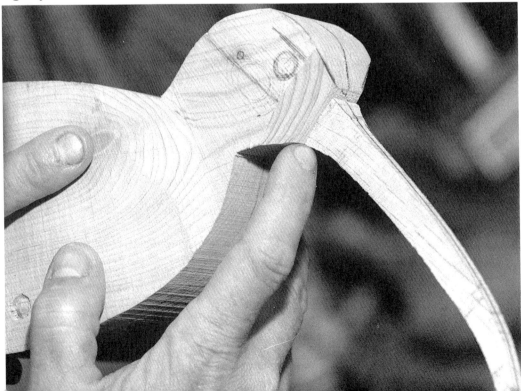

Mark carves the bill with a large skew chisel. "This tool might appear to be a bit much for the job," says Mark, "but if you look at the tip of the skew, it's actually a little knife. Instead of pecking away with a knife, I prefer to use the skew because of its weight and leverage. You can use two hands and get a lot of control with it."

After being rounded with the skew chisel, the bill is faired with the rasp.

"The rasp helps create an infinite number of smooth, flowing lines," says Mark. He uses it along the junction between the bill and head to make a pleasing transition between the two, giving the impression that the bill and head are naturally fused.

The half-round side of the rasp is used to create a slightly concave eye channel, which is carried across to the top of the bill.

"White oak is a very handsome wood and finishes beautifully with a knife," Mark says. "I get the shape I want with the rasp, but I smooth it with a carving knife."

Now Mark is ready to lock the mortise and tenon joint in position with a small spline. First he draws a pencil line through the tenon perpendicular with the grain of the head. The spline will be inserted along this line; if it were inserted parallel to the grain of the wood, it could act as a wedge and cause the wood to split.

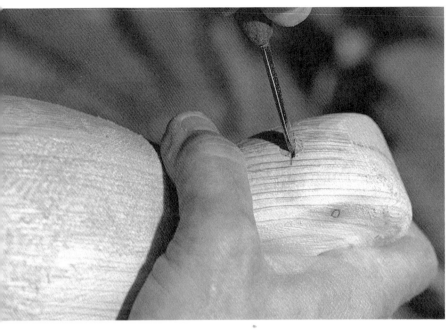

The knife is used to cut a narrow channel across the tenon that will accept the spline.

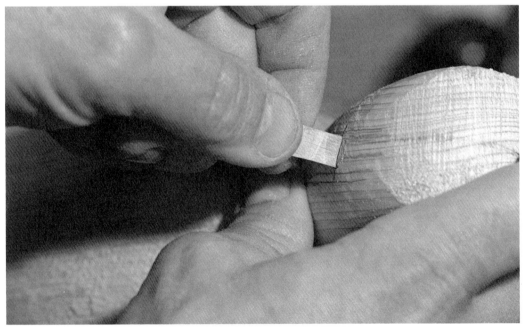

The tapered spline of white oak (salvaged from earlier roughing-out steps on the bandsaw) is inserted into the channel.

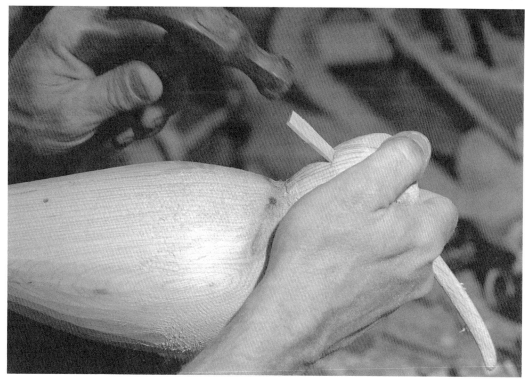

Mark uses a light hammer to gently tap the spline into position.

The spline is cut off flush with the back of the head.

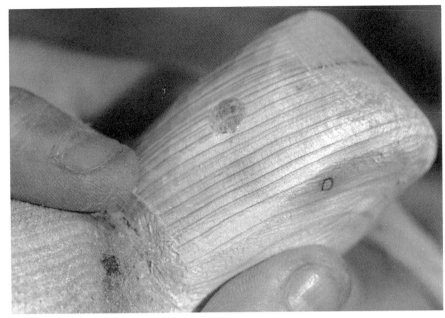

The finished joint is tight and the bill now is affixed permanently. This technique provides a strong, precise fit without the need for glue.

Mark McNair's finished curlew bill and head, ready for painting.

4

Martin Gates
Carving an Eagle Beak in Walnut

Until 1987, Martin Gates had never carved a bird for competition. He had worked in his father's antique shop near Gainesville, Florida, restoring European antiques, and he had taken up carving part time after spending two months as an apprentice to Dan DeMendoza, a Florida artist who specializes in miniatures.

But in 1987 a fellow employee at the antique shop who happened to be a carver and member of the Ward Foundation talked Martin into entering the Ward World Championship Carving Competition in Ocean City, Maryland. It was the first year for World Class entries in interpretive sculpture, and Martin did an elaborate carving of an egret, a common wading bird in central Florida. The bird won the $6,000 first-place award in World Class, and Martin was launched on a full-time carving career.

Since that Cinderella-like beginning, Martin has won many major prizes and has been invited to show his work in the most prestigious exhibitions in the country. In addition to his Ward Competition wins, Martin has won at the Grand Masters Competition and at the Gulf-South in New Orleans, and he has been in such heralded juried exhibitions as the Birds in Art show at the Leigh Yawkey Woodson Art Museum in Wausau, Wisconsin, the Southeastern Wildlife Art Exposition in Charleston, the Easton Waterfowl Festival in Maryland, and the fall Ward Foundation exhibition in Salisbury.

In this session, Martin continues a project begun in volume three of this series when he carved the head of an eagle from a block of black walnut. Here, Martin moves to the beak of the bird, adding detail with a series of knives, chisels, and gouges. Martin carves slowly and painstakingly, and the only power tool he uses in the entire process is a chain saw to rough out the block. The remainder of the wood is removed slowly, a chip at a time, with a wide variety of hand tools.

The wood is a triple-crotch of black walnut that was seasoning in Martin's yard for more than two years. Martin wanted to carve an eagle as a tribute to all of those majestic birds, as well as other wildlife, that were lost in the 1989 Alaskan oil spill caused by the grounding of the tanker Exxon Valdez. He decided to carve the eagle in a calling position because he felt it represented the anguish the oil spill exacted on humans and wildlife alike.

As this session begins, the beak has been roughed out, and Martin will carve the ceres, the nostril, and will add detail to both the inside and outside of the opened beak. He uses photographs as reference, then draws paper patterns to achieve the correct proportions and scale.

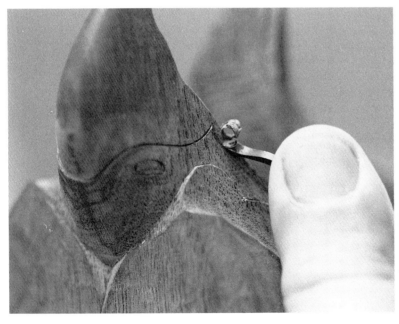

Martin scribes a line to separate the fleshy ceres from the beak, then uses a small bent chisel to remove wood from the ceres.

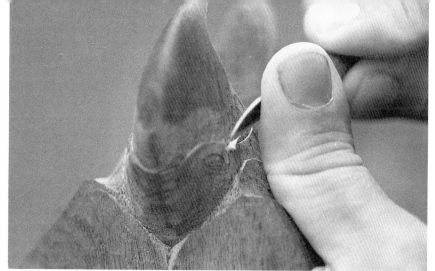

A knife is used to trim wood from the beak. Martin uses no power tools—only well-sharpened knives, chisels, and gouges—and the carving process is time-consuming. He removes a small amount of wood from both sides of the beak and ceres, being sure to keep the proportions and balance correct.

Martin has an extensive collection of chisels and gouges, many of which are antique tools purchased in Europe. He uses this small chisel to define the line separating the beak and the ceres.

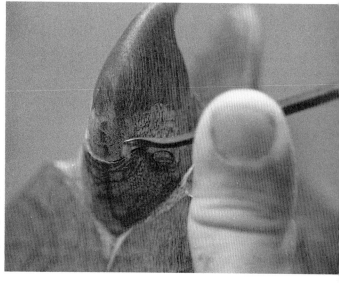

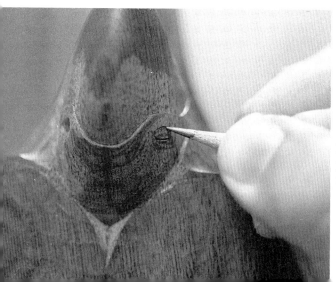

Martin uses a sharp pencil to determine the position of the nostrils. Using photographs to guide him, Martin sketches the nostrils onto the walnut, changing the position slightly until he is satisfied with the location. "With a pencil you can keep erasing until you have them just right," he says. "Once you make the cut, it's too late."

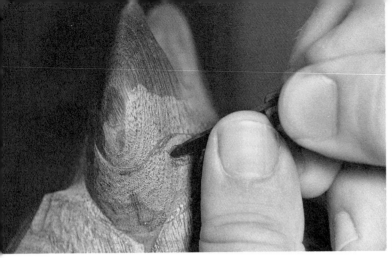

Martin uses a small knife
to outline the nostril,
following the pencil marks
he just made.

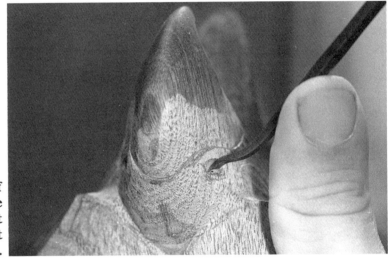

With the outline of
the nostril cut, he
uses a small bent
gouge to scoop out
the wood.

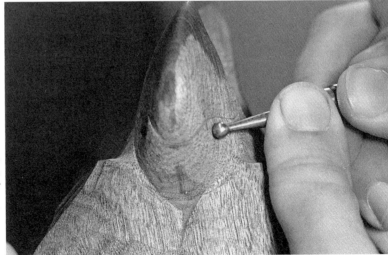

A round burnishing tool
is used to soften the edges
of the nostril, rounding off
the opening slightly.

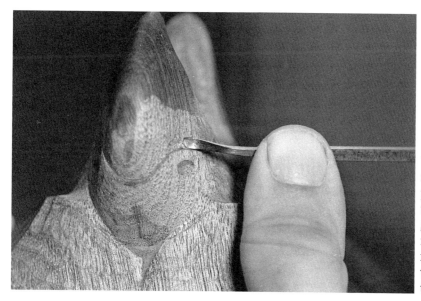

With the right nostril completed, Martin uses the bent gouge to remove more wood from the bill where it meets the ceres.

A larger curved gouge is used to trim the edge of the ceres. "You have to keep going over it several times to get it the way you want it," says Martin.

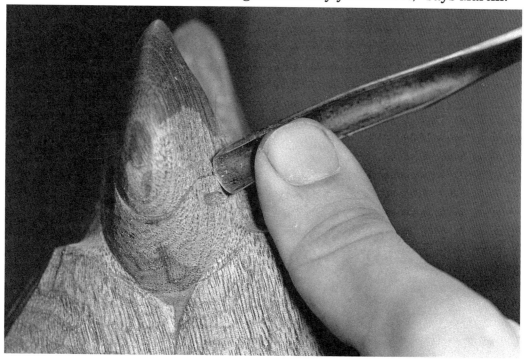

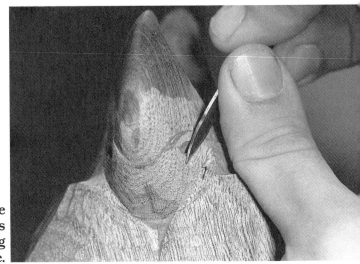

With a knife he levels off the ceres and removes the cut marks left by the small gouge, creating a clean surface.

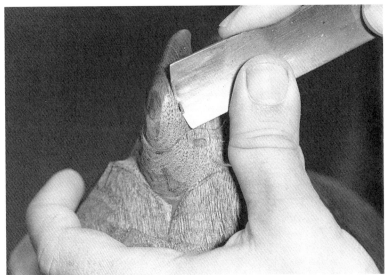

A large, shallow gouge is used to create the small indentation in the bill just forward of the nostril. Martin makes extensive use of close-up photographs when adding detail such as this.

The small bent gouge is used to bevel the edge of the ceres.

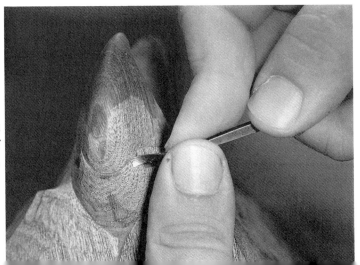

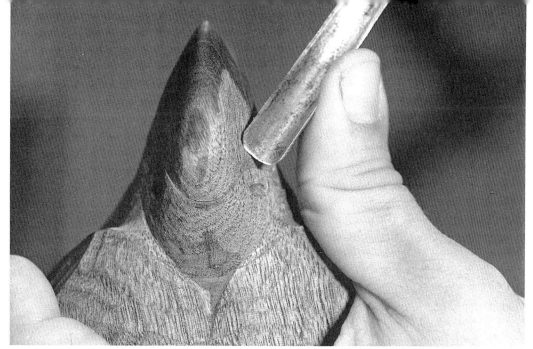

The larger bent gouge is used to remove more wood from the indentation in the bill. "I keep going back and forth from one area to another," says Martin. "With this type of carving, you don't necessarily complete one area then go to the next. What you do in one area affects an area adjacent to it. So you keep working on many aspects at the same time, bringing them along together."

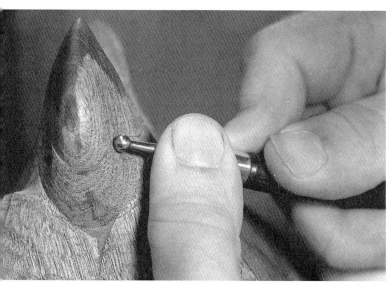

When Martin is satisfied with the right side of the bill, he uses the burnishing tool to finish the area. The burnishing tool depresses the wood fibers and produces a hard, somewhat glossy surface.

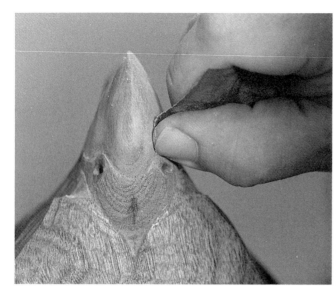

Fine sandpaper (150- to 220-grit) is used to finish the surface. The tools leave a fairly smooth finish, and little sanding is required.

Martin carves the inside and the outside of the bill simultaneously, removing wood from both sides until he achieves the correct outside dimension and the correct thickness. He uses a spoon gouge to remove wood from the throat of the eagle.

Martin now goes to the top of the bill, where he uses a knife to shape the beak.

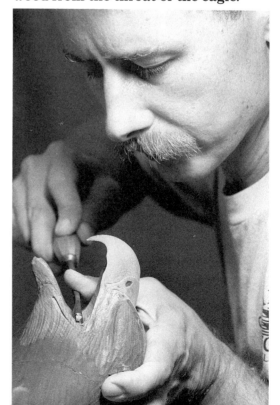

70

He removes as much wood from the throat as the length of his tools will allow.

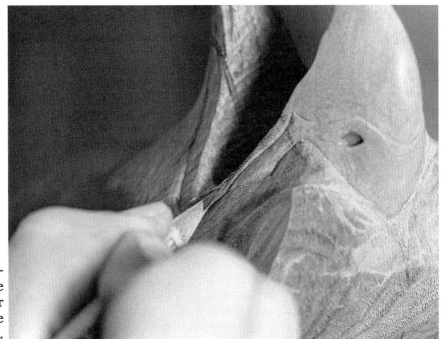

Martin uses a pencil to sketch the thin membrane, or "lip," at the corner of the beak.

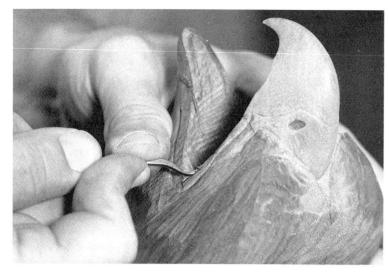

Then a small bent gouge is used to shape the membrane, following the pencil line drawn in the previous step.

The bent gouge is used to further hollow out the throat and make the opening deeper.

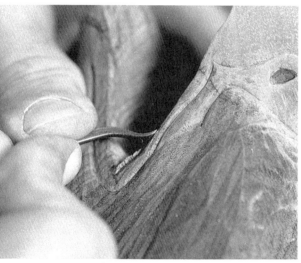

The same bent gouge is used to slightly bevel, or round off, the edge of the membrane along the base of the beak.

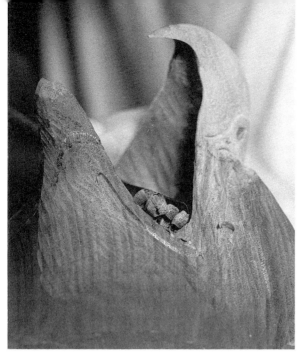

As Martin hollows out the bill, he leaves a thickness of approximately one-quarter inch within the mandible. This area will be thinned out after the outside of the bill is completed.

Top view of the head and bill; the head has been roughed out and the top of the bill is near completion. The next step is to finish detailing the lower beak and to carve the tongue.

A quarter-inch flat chisel is used to round off the bottom of the upper beak.

73

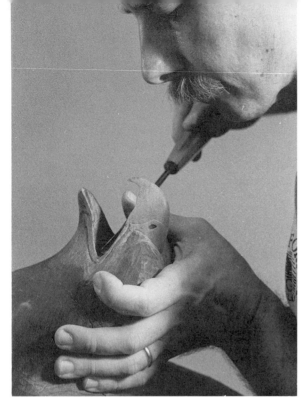

Again, the spoon gouge is used to hollow out the mouth. Martin alternates work between the inside and outside of the bill, taking care to maintain symmetry between the left and right sides.

Before beginning a carving, Martin makes a paper pattern of the entire bird. This ensures that as he carves, he maintains the correct proportion between different sections of the bird. As he works on the bill, he frequently checks the work against his paper template. Here he compares the lower bill to the pattern. At this point, the size and proportion of the bill are just about right; now more detail must be added.

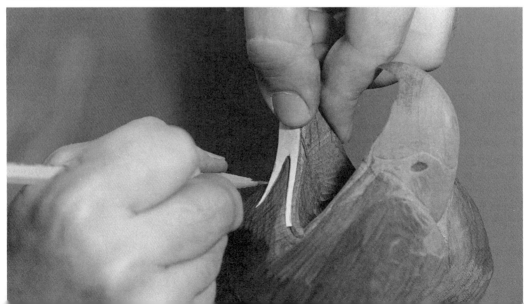

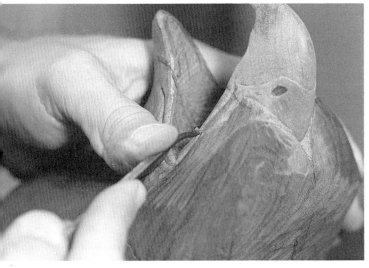

Here he uses the small bent gouge to deepen the lines along the edge of the bill.

The same gouge is used to shape the bottom of the beak. It will be narrowed slightly so it will give the impression of fitting into the upper beak.

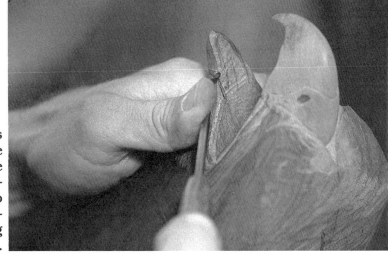

The edge of the bill is rounded with the quarter-inch chisel.

The bent gouge is used to shape the membrane at the base of the beak where the upper and lower mandibles meet.

Martin then uses a small spoon gouge to begin carving the inside of the beak where the mandibles meet.

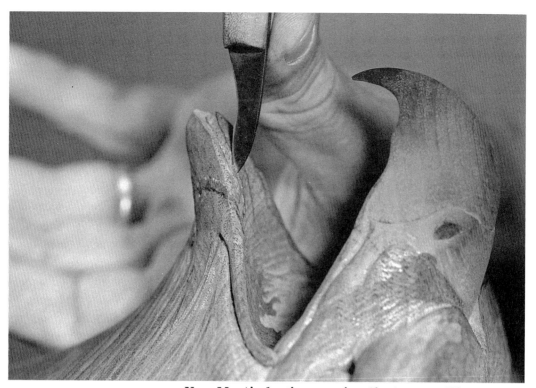

Now Martin begins carving the tongue. The tongue will not have a great deal of detail, but it must be separated slightly from the lower mandible, and it should have a shallow groove running lengthwise down the center. He starts by outlining the tongue with a sharp knife.

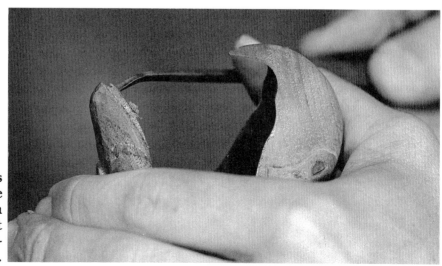

After the tongue is defined with the knife cuts, Martin uses the bent gouge to undercut it.

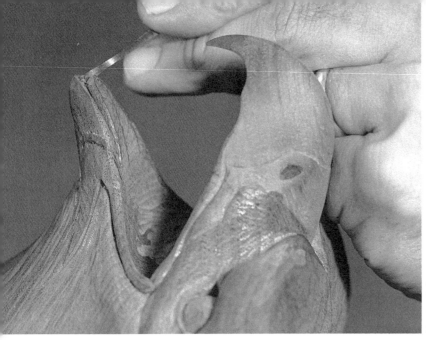

A small gouge is used
to remove wood around
the tongue, defining
its shape.

When the tongue is shaped, the same gouge is
used to remove a small amount of wood beneath it,
giving the impression that the tongue is raised.

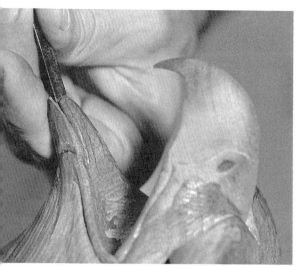

Martin uses a shallow gouge to clean and smooth the area beneath the tongue. This tool removes most of the marks left by the small gouges.

He relieves the sides of the tongue with the bent gouge by cutting a slight line along its sides.

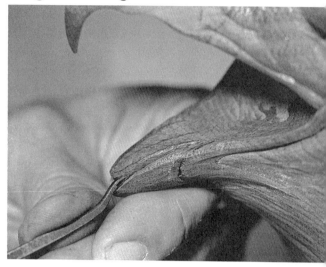

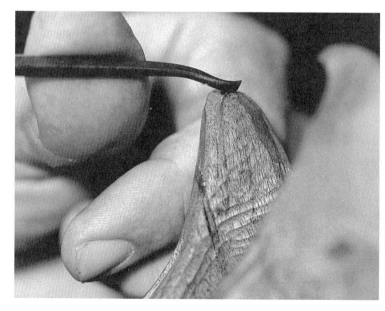

He uses the same tool to slightly bevel the edge of the tongue, rounding it off.

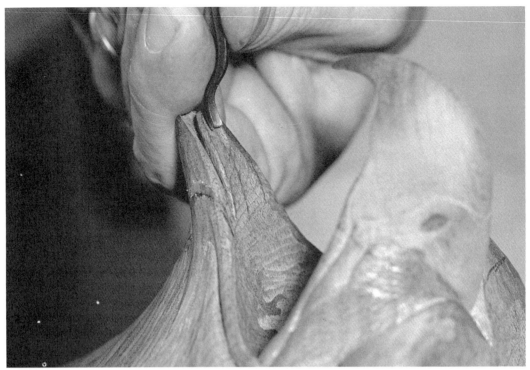

Martin carves a slight groove along the length of the tongue with the bent gouge. Detail doesn't have to be as exact on an interpretive sculpture as it would on a realistic bird, but he must use enough detail to show that the bird is calling. A slight groove along the tongue, coupled with a lifting of the tip of the tongue, should suffice.

As the bill nears completion, Martin again checks the lower mandible against the paper pattern. Some wood in the throat area still needs to be removed.

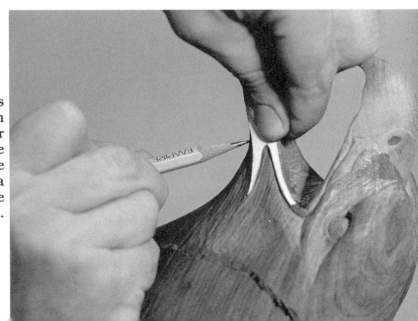

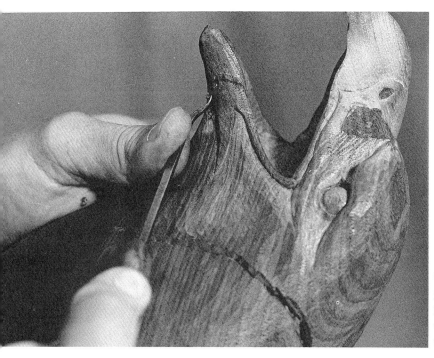

The bent gouge
is used to finish the
lower mandible
where the bill meets
the head.

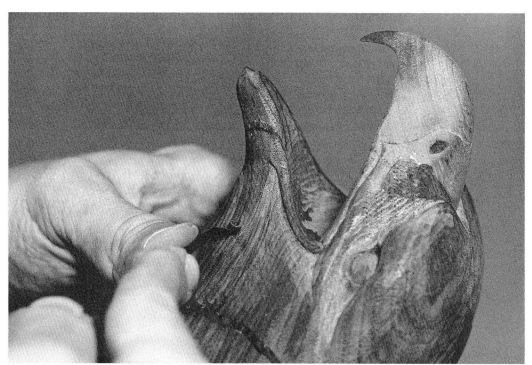

Martin also uses it to remove wood along the neck
area, making it conform to the pattern.

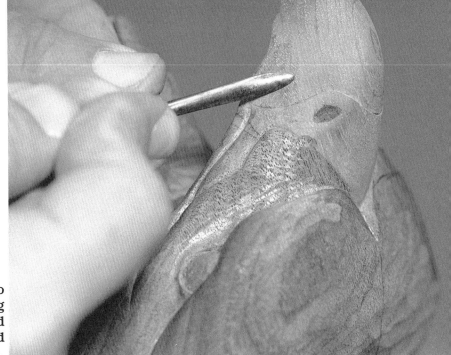

The final step is to use a burnishing tool to polish and compact the wood fibers of the beak.

The completed head of the eagle.

About the Author

Curtis Badger has written widely about wildfowl art, wildfowl hunting, and conservation issues in general. His articles have appeared in many national and regional magazines, and he serves as editor of *Wildfowl Art Journal,* which is published by the Ward Foundation. He is currently working with carver Jim Sprankle on a book on wildfowl painting techniques, and he is writing a book about growing up on the Virginia coast. He lives in Onley, Virginia.

Other Books of Interest to Bird Carvers

Songbird Carving with Ernest Muehlmatt
Muehlmatt shares his expertise on painting, washes, feather flicking, and burning, plus insights on composition, design, proportion, and balance.

Waterfowl Carving with J. D. Sprankle
A fully illustrated reference to carving and painting 25 decorative ducks.

Carving Miniature Wildfowl with Robert Guge
Scale drawings, step-by-step photographs, and painting keys demonstrate the techniques that make Guge's miniatures the best in the world.

Decorative Decoy Designs
Bruce Burk's two volumes (*Dabbling and Whistling Ducks* and *Diving Ducks*) are complete guides to decoy painting by a renowned master of the art. Both feature life-size color patterns, reference photographs, alternate position patterns, and detailed paint-mixing instructions for male and female of twelve duck species.

Bird Carving Basics: Eyes
Volume one in the series presents a variety of techniques on how to insert glass eyes, carve and paint wooden eyes, burn, carve with and without fillers, and suggest detail. Featured carvers include Jim Sprankle, Lee Osborne, Pete Peterson, and Grayson Chesser.

Bird Carving Basics: Feet
Volume two features the same spectacular photography and detailed step-by-step format. Techniques for making feet out of wood, metal, and epoxy, creating texture and tone, and shaping feet in various positions are demonstrated by Dan Brown, Jo Craemer, and Larry Tawes, Jr.

Bird Carving Basics: Heads
Volume three illustrates how to create realistic head feathers by various methods, such as burning, wrinkling, stoning, and carving flow lines. Experts like Jim Sprankle, Mark McNair, and Martin Gates share their innovative techniques.

For ordering information and a complete list of carving titles, write:
Stackpole Books
P.O. Box 1831
Harrisburg, PA 17105
or call 1-800-READ-NOW

BIRDS OF A FEATHER

BIRD CARVING BASICS
AND
WILDFOWL CARVING & COLLECTING MAGAZINE

A quarterly magazine for bird carving enthusiasts!
- how-to demos
- full-color reference photos
- Beginner's Notebook, interviews, and much, much more!

If you carve wildfowl,

you can't be without
WILDFOWL CARVING & COLLECTING MAGAZINE,
the only regular publication
serving the bird carving
community.

Send for your *free* information today!